TOSEL®
READING SERIES

JUNIOR

READING

3

ITC International TOSEL Committee

CONTENTS

About TOSEL®

TOSEL (Test of Skills in the English Language) was developed to meet the demand for a more effective assessment of English as a foreign language for learners from specific cultural settings.

TOSEL evaluates and certifies the proficiency levels of English learners, from the age of 4 through adulthood, along with academic and job performance results.

Background

- Other English tests are ineffective in accurately measuring individual abilities
- Overuse of US-dominated testing systems in diverse cultural and educational contexts in the global English language learning market

Functions & Usage

- Assessment is categorized into 7 levels
- Used as a qualification for academic excellence for school admissions
- Used as a test to assess the English proficiency in the corporate and public sectors

Goals

- Create an effective tool for assessing and evaluating the English skills of English language learners
- Implement efficient and accessible testing systems and methods
- Provide constructive and developmental English education guidance

TOSEL® Strength

LEVELED ASSESSMENTS

An established English test system fit for seven different levels according to learners' cognitive development

ACCURATE DIAGNOSIS

A systematic and scientific diagnosis of learners' English proficiency

EXTENSIVE MATERIALS

Supplementary materials to help learners in an EFL environment to prepare for TOSEL and improve their proficiency

SUFFICIENT DATA

Content for each level developed by using data accumulated from more than 2,000,000 TOSEL test takers delegated at 15,000 schools and academies

CLASSIFIED AREAS OF INTELLIGENCE

Content designed to foster and expand the strengths of each student, categorized by the eight areas of intelligence

CONTINUITY

A complete course of English education ranging from kindergarten, elementary school, middle school, high schoool, and up to adults.

HIGH RELIABILITY

A high reliability level (Cronbach's alpha: .904 for elementary school students / .864 for university students) proven by several studies (Oxford University / Modern Language Journal)

SYSTEMATIC & EFFECTIVE ENGLISH EDUCATION

Accurate diagnosis and extensive materials which provide a step-by-step development in English learning, according to the quality of each learner's ability

TOSEL® Level Chart

Seven Separate Assessments

TOSEL divides the test into seven stages, by considering the test takers' cognitive levels, according to different ages. Unlike other assessments based on only one level, TOSEL includes separate assessments for preschool, elementary school, middle school, high school students, and for adults, which also includes both professionals and college students.

TOSEL's reporting system highlights the strengths and weaknesses of each test taker and suggests areas for further development.

COCOON

Suitable for children aged 4-6 (pre-schoolers)

The first step in the TOSEL system, the test is composed of colorful designs and interesting questions to interest young learners and to put them at ease.

Pre-STARTER

Suitable for children aged 7-8 (1st-2nd grades of elementary school)

Evaluates the ability to comprehend simple vocabulary, conversations, and sentences.

STARTER

Suitable for children aged 9-10 (3rd-4th grades of elementary school)

Evaluates the ability to comprehend short sentences and conversations related to everyday situations or topics.

BASIC

Suitable for children aged 11-12 (5th–6th grades of elementary school)

Evaluates the ability to communicate about personal information, daily activities, future plans, and past experiences in written and spoken language.

JUNIOR

Suitable for middle school students

Evaluates the ability to comprehend short paragraphs, practical texts, and speech covering general topics and to participate in simple daily conversations.

HIGH JUNIOR

Suitable for high school students

Evaluates the ability to use English fluently, accurately, and effectively on a wide range of social and academic subjects, as well as the ability to use sentences with a variety of complex structures.

ADVANCED

Suitable for university students and adults

Evaluates the ability to use practical English required for a job or work environment, as well as the ability to use and understand English at the university level.

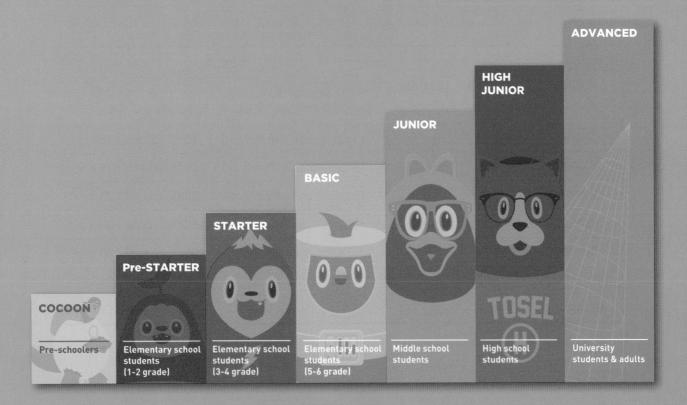

Evaluation

Assessing the Four Skills

TOSEL evaluates the four language skills: reading, listening, speaking and writing, through indirect and direct assessment items.

This system of evaluation is part of a concerted effort to break away from materials geared solely toward grammar and reading-oriented education.

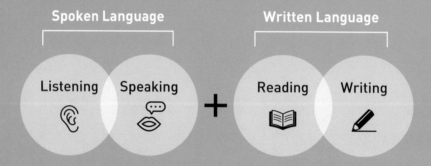

TOSEL Test Information

Level	Score	Grade	Section	
			Section I Listening & Speaking	Section II Reading & Writing
COCOON	100		15 Questions / 15 min	15 Questions / 15 min
Pre-STARTER	100		15 Questions / 15 min	20 Questions / 25 min
STARTER	100		20 Questions / 15 min	20 Questions / 25 min
BASIC	100	1-10	30 Questions / 20 min	30 Questions / 30 min
JUNIOR	100		30 Questions / 20 min	30 Questions / 30 min
HIGH JUNIOR	100		30 Questions / 25 min	35 Questions / 35 min
ADVANCED	990		70 Questions / 45 min	70 Questions / 55 min

Certificates

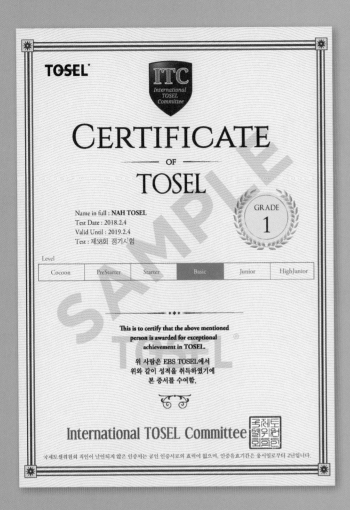

TOSEL Certificate

The International TOSEL Committee officially evaluates and certifies the level of English proficiency of English learners from the age of 4 to adults.

Certified by

Mar. 2010   Korea University
Dec. 2009   The Korean Society of Speech Science
Dec. 2009   The Korea Association of Foreign Language Education
Nov. 2009   The Applied Linguistics Association of Korea
Oct. 2009   The Pan Korea English Teachers Association

CHAPTER 1

Famous People 1

UNIT 1

Linus Pauling

Have you ever heard of Linus Pauling?
Look at the illustration.
What do you think Pauling was known for?

Linus Pauling loved chemistry from a very young age. When he was still in junior high school in Oregon, USA, Pauling and his friends did experiments after school. They would go to a nearby factory looking for materials to practice chemistry. In university, Linus Pauling continued to study chemistry, and eventually became a professor. He mostly researched how the molecules of different chemicals bond together. His research is still studied today and was so important that Pauling won a Nobel Prize in chemistry in 1954. However, he was not just well known because of his scientific achievements. He also worked very hard to bring peace to the world. Throughout his life, he talked about the need to stop all wars. He believed that all wars are bad. In particular, he was against nuclear weapons, thinking that they were too dangerous to use. Many people disagreed with him, and even the government sometimes disliked what he said, but he continued to speak about how terrible war is. In 1962, Linus Pauling won the Nobel Peace Prize. This made him the second person to win two Nobel Prizes after scientist Marie Curie.

New Words

chemistry

n science that studies what things are made of

experiment

n a controlled science procedure

material

n something that can be used to make something else

molecule

n a group of atoms

disagree with X

v have a different opinion from X

nuclear weapon

n a bomb that uses energy from the center of atoms to make an explosion

Part A. Sentence Completion

1. A: How is your science class?
    B: Good, but difficult. Some of the readings are _____ understand.

    (A) too hard
    (B) too hard to
    (C) as hard to we
    (D) as to hard we

2. A: I thought that presenter was great!
    B: He was interesting, but I don't really _____ him.

    (A) agree
    (B) agree by
    (C) agree for
    (D) agree with

Part B. Situational Writing

3.

I love all my classes, but my favorite subject is _____.

    (A) statistics
    (B) chemistry
    (C) astronomy
    (D) economics

4.

There are debates about _____.

    (A) acid rain
    (B) animal rights
    (C) water pollution
    (D) nuclear weapons

Tonight! ——— Live on Television!

Two Speakers

Edward Teller

- Physicist
- Co-creator of atomic bombs
- Worked on hydrogen bombs

Position: Nuclear weapons can help to prevent a third world war. And damage from nuclear fallout may not be as bad as other radioactivity.

Linus Pauling

- Chemist
- Is against the continued development of nuclear weapons

Position: Nuclear weapons should not be developed as a way to prevent war. Damage from nuclear fallout is severe.

5.   What is the notice most likely for?

   (A)   a book
   (B)   a radio show
   (C)   a sports match
   (D)   a debate on TV

6.   According to the notice, what is true?

   (A)   Teller helped shut down a nuclear power plant.
   (B)   Pauling proved that nuclear fallout was not severe.
   (C)   Teller argues nuclear weapons can help prevent war.
   (D)   Pauling shows why nuclear weapons should be developed.

Part D. General Reading and Retelling

Linus Pauling loved chemistry from a very young age. When he was still in junior high school in Oregon, USA, Pauling and his friends did experiments after school. They would go to a nearby factory looking for materials to practice chemistry. In university, Linus Pauling continued to study chemistry, and eventually became a professor. He mostly researched how the molecules of different chemicals bond together. His research is still studied today and was so important that Pauling won a Nobel Prize in chemistry in 1954. However, he was not just well known because of his scientific achievements. He also worked very hard to bring peace to the world. Throughout his life, he talked about the need to stop all wars. He believed that all wars are bad. In particular, he was against nuclear weapons, thinking that they were too dangerous to use. Many people disagreed with him, and even the government sometimes disliked what he said, but he continued to speak about how terrible war is. In 1962, Linus Pauling won the Nobel Peace Prize. This made him the second person to win two Nobel Prizes after scientist Marie Curie.

7. Which is the best title for the passage?

   (A) Linus Pauling: Biochemist and Soldier
   (B) Linus Pauling: Chemist and Peace Activist
   (C) Linus Pauling: Inventor of Nuclear Weapons
   (D) Linus Pauling: 18th Century Chemistry Expert

8. According to the passage, what did Pauling do as a child?

   (A) work in a chemical plant
   (B) make weapons for his country
   (C) look for materials from a local factory
   (D) injure an eye in a chemistry experiment

9. Which of the following is mentioned about Pauling?

   (A) his wife
   (B) his friends
   (C) his children
   (D) his mentors

10. According to the passage, which of the following statements would Pauling most likely agree with?

   (A) "Humans need to go to war sometimes."
   (B) "War is never the right choice for the world."
   (C) "Chemistry's purpose is to help the military."
   (D) "At least nuclear weapons are safer than other ones."

Listening Practice

 Listen and write.

  MP3 J3-1

Linus Pauling

Linus Pauling loved ¹_____ from a very young age. When he was still in junior high school in Oregon, USA, Pauling and his friends did ²_____ after school. They would go to a nearby factory looking for ³_____ to practice chemistry. In university, Linus Pauling continued to study chemistry, and eventually became a professor. He mostly researched how the ⁴_____ of different chemicals bond together. His research is still studied today and was so important that Pauling won a Nobel Prize in chemistry in 1954. However, he was not just well known because of his scientific achievements. He also worked very hard to bring peace to the world. Throughout his life, he talked about the need to stop all wars. He believed that all wars are bad. In particular, he was against ⁵_____ weapons, thinking that they were too dangerous to use. Many people ⁶_____ with him, and even the government sometimes disliked what he said, but he continued to speak about how terrible war is. In 1962, Linus Pauling won the Nobel Peace Prize. This made him the second person to win two Nobel Prizes after scientist Marie Curie.

Word Bank

molicules	experiments	nucular
molecules	materials	disagreement
expiriments	nuclear	chemistry
cemistry	disagreed	matterials

 Listen. Pause. Say each sentence.

  MP3 J3-1G

Writing Practice

  Write the words.

1 _____

n science that studies what things are made of

2 _____

n a controlled science procedure

3 _____

n something that can be used to make something else

4 _____

n a group of atoms

5 _____ **X**

v have a different opinion from X

6 _____

n a bomb that uses energy from the center of atoms to make an explosion

  Write the words in each blank.

Summary

Linus Pauling's _____ research was so important that he won a _____ Prize. He also spoke against wars and _____ weapons, even though many people _____ with him.

Word Puzzle

  Complete the word puzzle.

1 →
a controlled science procedure

2 ↓
a bomb that uses energy from the center of atoms to make an explosion

3 ↓
have a different opinion from X

5 →
something that can be used to make something else

6 →
a group of atoms

4 ↓
science that studies what things are made of

UNIT 2

Maryam Mirzakhani

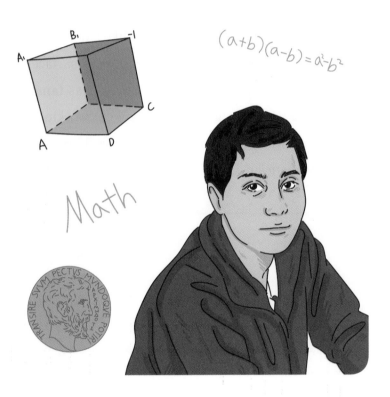

Have you ever heard of Maryam Mirzakhani?
Look at the illustration.
What do you think Mirzakhani was known for?

Maryam Mirzakhani was an incredible person in the world of mathematics. She was famous for a variety of reasons. First, she was the only woman ever to win the Fields Medal. Sixty people have won the award so far. Except for Mirzakhani, they have all been male. Second, Mirzakhani was the first person from Iran to win it. In doing so, she reminded the world of Iran's long tradition of mathematics. Third, Mirzakhani's work was fascinating to mathematicians all over the globe. As a mathematician, Mirzakhani thought of many confusing problems and aimed to find solutions. She worked in a difficult area of geometry and studied imaginary surfaces. The surfaces she studied were both curved like a wavy potato chip and closed like a doughnut. She also explored the movement of shapes like billiard balls. Her ideas about surfaces helped lead other mathematicians to new questions. Fourth, Mirzakhani was famous for her bravery in the face of illness. Even when she got cancer, she kept working on her research. In short, Maryam Mirzakhani will be remembered by the world for her incredible work as a ground-breaking mathematician.

New Words

geometry

n mathematics that studies shapes

fascinating

adj very interesting

imaginary

adj not real, only in your mind

surface

n a top layer of an object

billiard ball

n a ball in a sport with a wooden stick and a green table

ground-breaking

adj very important because it is the first

Part A. Sentence Completion

1. A: Did you read that book I recommended?
   B: I did, and I found it really _____.

   (A) fascinate
   (B) fascinator
   (C) fascinated
   (D) fascinating

2. A: Did she win the award?
   B: She did! Sixty people _____ it so far, but she's the first woman.

   (A) win
   (B) won
   (C) wins
   (D) have won

Part B. Situational Writing

3.

   Ms. Parva teaches the _____ class.

   (A) biology
   (B) anatomy
   (C) literature
   (D) geometry

4.

   There are seven _____ balls on the table.

   (A) billiard
   (B) basket
   (C) striped
   (D) sunken

Day Camp Schedule

Day	Monday	Tuesday	Wednesday	Thursday	Friday
Course	"Life of Pi"	"Awesome Geometry"	"Life of Pi"	"Awesome Geometry"	"Project Sharing"

All workshops: 10:00 AM to noon

"Life of Pi" ——————— Do fun activities related to the number pi!

"Awesome Geometry" —— Learn about the incredible work of Dr. Maryam Mirzakhani. Study her proofs on how billiard balls could work!

"Project Sharing" ——— On Monday, you choose your own project to work on. On Friday, enjoy a showcase of all the projects.

5. What kind of camp is this most likely to be?

(A) math
(B) sports
(C) theater
(D) chemistry

6. Which would campers most likely do at the camp?

(A) stay overnight on a Thursday in a forest cabin
(B) arrive for geometry lessons on Tuesday afternoon
(C) do a task with the number 3.14 on a Wednesday morning
(D) present a finished project on billiard balls on Friday evening

Part D. General Reading and Retelling

Maryam Mirzakhani was an incredible person in the world of mathematics. She was famous for a variety of reasons. First, she was the only woman ever to win the Fields Medal. Sixty people have won the award so far. Except for Mirzakhani, they have all been male. Second, Mirzakhani was the first person from Iran to win it. In doing so, she reminded the world of Iran's long tradition of mathematics. Third, Mirzakhani's work was fascinating to mathematicians all over the globe. As a mathematician, Mirzakhani thought of many confusing problems and aimed to find solutions. She worked in a difficult area of geometry and studied imaginary surfaces. The surfaces she studied were both curved like a wavy potato chip and closed like a doughnut. She also explored the movement of shapes like billiard balls. Her ideas about surfaces helped lead other mathematicians to new questions. Fourth, Mirzakhani was famous for her bravery in the face of illness. Even when she got cancer, she kept working on her research. In short, Maryam Mirzakhani will be remembered by the world for her incredible work as a ground-breaking mathematician.

7. What is the passage mainly about?

   (A) difficulties Maryam Mirzakhani faced in life
   (B) how Maryam Mirzakhani succeeded in Iran
   (C) Maryam Mirzakhani's work on curing cancer
   (D) four reasons Maryam Mirzakhani was famous

8. Which of the following is NOT mentioned about Mirzakhani?

   (A) books she liked
   (B) a prize she won
   (C) her home country
   (D) a disease she had

9. What subject did Mirzakhani focus on?

   (A) sports
   (B) nutrition
   (C) geometry
   (D) economics

10. According to the passage, which of the following did Mirzakhani do?

   (A) become a politician
   (B) invent a new kind of potato chip
   (C) consider how billiard balls move
   (D) graduate from university at the age of ten

Listening Practice

 Listen and write.

  ▶ MP3 J3-2

Maryam Mirzakhani

Maryam Mirzakhani was an incredible person in the world of mathematics. She was famous for a variety of reasons. First, she was the only woman ever to win the Fields Medal. Sixty people have won the award so far. Except for Mirzakhani, they have all been male. Second, Mirzakhani was the first person from Iran to win it. In doing so, she reminded the world of Iran's long tradition of mathematics. Third, Mirzakhani's work was ¹ _____ to mathematicians all over the globe. As a mathematician, Mirzakhani thought of many confusing problems and aimed to find solutions. She worked in a difficult area of ² _____ and studied ³ _____ surfaces. The ⁴ _____ she studied were both curved like a wavy potato chip and closed like a doughnut. She also explored the movement of shapes like ⁵ _____ balls. Her ideas about surfaces helped lead other mathematicians to new questions. Fourth, Mirzakhani was famous for her bravery in the face of illness. Even when she got cancer, she kept working on her research. In short, Maryam Mirzakhani will be remembered by the world for her incredible work as a ⁶ _____ mathematician.

Word Bank

surfaces	ground-breaking	fascinating
imaginarry	biliard	geometry
imaginary	fascinated	surface
billiard	ground-braking	geomatry

 Listen. Pause. Say each sentence.

  ▶ MP3 J3-2G

Writing Practice

 Write the words.

1 _____

  n mathematics that studies shapes

2 _____

  adj very interesting

3 _____

  adj not real, only in your mind

4 _____

  n a top layer of an object

5 _____

  n a ball in a sport with a wooden stick and a green table

6 _____

  adj very important because it is the first

 Write the words in each blank.

Summary

Ground-breaking _____ Maryam Mirzakhani was the only woman ever to win the Fields _____ and the _____ Iranian to win it. She continued her fascinating research even when she got _____ .

Complete the word puzzle.

1 ↓
a ball in a sport with a wooden stick and a green table

2 ↓
very important because it is the first

3 →
not real, only in your mind

4 ↓
mathematics that studies shapes

5 →
a top layer of an object

6 →
very interesting

UNIT 3

CV Raman

Teacher's Book
p.182

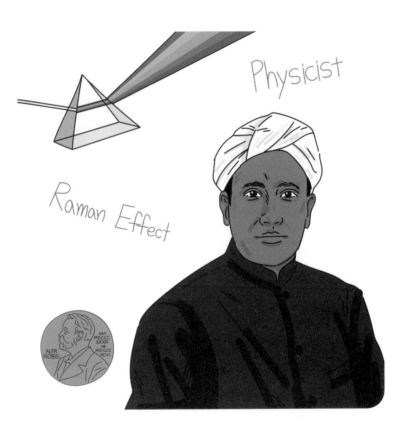

Have you ever heard of CV Raman?
Look at the illustration.
What do you think Raman was known for?

Sir Chandrasekhara Venkata Raman, better known as C.V. Raman, was a scientist born in India in 1888. He advanced in his education very quickly, beginning high school at the age of eleven. By thirteen, he had finished high school and received a scholarship to go to university. When he was only sixteen, Raman graduated with a university degree in physics, and three years later earned his master's degree. As a professor at the University of Calcutta, Raman studied how light reacts when it goes through a clear object. Most light goes straight through, but some of the light changes direction. This discovery helped prove that light is made of small particles called "photons." The research Raman did was so revolutionary that he won the Nobel Prize for Physics in 1930, and the changes to light when it goes through a clear object are called the "Raman effect." Raman continued to work on his research with light and sound but also used his success to provide opportunities for other people. He helped establish many research institutes in India so that other young, bright students could make new discoveries in science.

New Words

advance
v   go to the next level

scholarship
n   money given to students to help them go to (or pay for) school

particle
n   a tiny piece of something

revolutionary
adj   ground-breaking

establish
v   create

institute
n   a place for education

Part A. Sentence Completion

1. A: What an incredible musician!
    B: Yeah. She gave her first concert at the age _____ four.

    (A) in
    (B) of
    (C) at
    (D) for

2. A: What did this experiment prove?
    B: It proved that light _____ up of different parts.

    (A) made
    (B) making
    (C) is made
    (D) is making

Part B. Situational Writing

3.

Meena has been offered a _____ for school.

    (A) trophy
    (B) uniform
    (C) highlighter
    (D) scholarship

4.

If you get past the dragon, you _____ the rainbow level.

    (A) part from
    (B) advance to
    (C) fall between
    (D) remain before

This Certificate of Scientific Excellence

is awarded to **Rosa Juarez**

for her outstanding performance at the 23rd Annual Firestone Physics Fair

this day of 12 July, 2020

at Firestone Community Hall for her project titled
"Light and Heat Absorption."

Signed: _____

Maria Rannells, President of the Firestone Physics Society

5. According to the certificate, who most likely is Rosa Juarez?

    (A) a participant at a science fair
    (B) a contestant in an art contest
    (C) the MVP in a baseball league
    (D) the president of a biology club

6. Which of the following is NOT mentioned?

    (A) the event date
    (B) the event place
    (C) the number of prizes
    (D) the name of the project

Part D. General Reading and Retelling

Sir Chandrasekhara Venkata Raman, better known as C.V. Raman, was a scientist born in India in 1888. He advanced in his education very quickly, beginning high school at the age of eleven. By thirteen, he had finished high school and received a scholarship to go to university. When he was only sixteen, Raman graduated with a university degree in physics, and three years later earned his master's degree. As a professor at the University of Calcutta, Raman studied how light reacts when it goes through a clear object. Most light goes straight through, but some of the light changes direction. This discovery helped prove that light is made of small particles called "photons." The research Raman did was so revolutionary that he won the Nobel Prize for Physics in 1930, and the changes to light when it goes through a clear object are called the "Raman effect." Raman continued to work on his research with light and sound but also used his success to provide opportunities for other people. He helped establish many research institutes in India so that other young, bright students could make new discoveries in science.

7. Which would be the best title for the passage?

(A) C.V. Raman: Peace Prize Winner
(B) C.V. Raman: From India to Europe
(C) A Physics Genius Called C.V. Raman
(D) A Math Specialist Named C.V. Raman

8. According to the passage, which of the following did Raman do?

(A) earn a master's degree when he was 19
(B) drop out of middle school when he was 16
(C) graduate from high school when he was 11
(D) receive a university scholarship when he was 17

9. According to the passage, what did Raman's discovery help prove?

(A) that outer space is dark
(B) that brains have neurons
(C) that most objects are clear
(D) that light is made of photons

10. What is the "Raman effect"?

(A) the changing of water into three forms
(B) the changing sound of an ambulance siren
(C) the changes to light going through a clear object
(D) the changes to prices when there is more demand

Listening Practice

 Listen and write.

 MP3 J3-3

CV Raman

Sir Chandrasekhara Venkata Raman, better known as C.V. Raman, was a scientist born in India in 1888. He ¹ _____ in his education very quickly, beginning high school at the age of eleven. By thirteen, he had finished high school and received a

² _____ to go to university. When he was only sixteen, Raman graduated with a university degree in physics, and three years later earned his master's degree. As a professor at the University of Calcutta, Raman studied how light reacts when it goes through a clear object. Most light goes straight through, but some of the light changes direction. This discovery helped prove that light is made of small ³ _____ called "photons." The research Raman did was so ⁴ _____ that he won the Nobel Prize for Physics in 1930, and the changes to light when it goes through a clear object are called the "Raman effect." Raman continued to work on his research with light and sound but also used his success to provide opportunities for other people. He helped ⁵ _____ many research ⁶ _____ in India so that other young, bright students could make new discoveries in science.

Word Bank

advance	established	institoots
advanced	establish	scholarship
scolarship	institutes	particles
revolutionary	revolutinary	particals

 Listen. Pause. Say each sentence.

 MP3 J3-3G

Writing Practice

 Write the words.

1 _____

　v　go to the next level

2 _____

　n　money given to students to help them go to (or pay for) school

3 _____

　n　a tiny piece of something

4 _____

　adj　ground-breaking

5 _____

　v　create

6 _____

　n　a place for education

 Write the words in each blank.

Summary

C.V. Raman, of India, discovered the "Raman _____", the changes light undergoes when it goes through a _____ object. This research was so _____ that he won the Nobel Prize for _____.

Word Puzzle

 Complete the word puzzle.

1 ↓
a tiny piece of something

2 ↓
money given to students to help them go to (or pay for) school

3 ↓
ground-breaking

5 ↓
a place for education

4 →
create

6 →
go to the next level

UNIT 4

Ada Lovelace

Have you ever heard of Ada Lovelace?
Look at the illustration.
What do you think Lovelace was known for?

Ada Lovelace, daughter of famous British poet Lord Byron, was born in 1815. From an early age, Lovelace's mother pushed her to study mathematics. Lovelace was often sick as a child, but that did not stop her from continuing her education. In the United Kingdom at the time, girls did not study much math and science in school. Only boys went to those classes. However, Lovelace's mother hired tutors to teach those subjects to her daughter at home. Lovelace had a deep passion for mathematics and studied university-level material on her own. At the age of 17, she met the inventor Charles Babbage. He taught her about his newest invention: the difference engine. This engine could solve math equations automatically when someone put in the numbers. Lovelace saw the potential of this engine, and suggested that it could be used to create automatic programs. Her research and comments on this topic directly led to simple versions of what we would eventually call "computers." During her life, many people did not know of her work, but in the 1950s, the world discovered how much she helped the beginning of development of computer technology. That is why now Ada Lovelace is called the world's "first computer programmer."

New Words

hire X *v* ask X to work for you	**subject** *n* a topic in school
have a deep passion for *v* care a lot about	**invention** *n* something new you created
automatically *adv* without humans doing it	**saw the potential of X** *v* thought X would later be useful or powerful

Part A. Sentence Completion

1. A: Why is Kelsie such a great runner?
    B: She never lets the heat stop _____.

    (A) her to running
    (B) to her running
    (C) from her running
    (D) her from running

2. A: What is this machine _____ for?
    B: It's for calculating numbers quickly.

    (A) use
    (B) used
    (C) using
    (D) to using

Part B. Situational Writing

3.

My brother got _____ as a nurse at the hospital.

(A) fired
(B) hired
(C) injured
(D) annoyed

4.

The caveman's new _____ is resting by his feet.

(A) bat
(B) footwear
(C) invention
(D) racehorse

Ada Lovelace Day Event

Ada Lovelace Day is celebrated all around the world on the second Tuesday in October. This year it is on October 13. Join us at this free event as we celebrate women in science, technology, engineering, and math.

6:30 to 9:00 PM   Kettering Events Hall

6:30-7:30 Talk by local computer science expert Dr. Fumiko Helmand
7:30-8:00 Performance by "math magician" Helena Pierce
8:00-9:00 Book signings, 3D printer demonstrations, and a hacking competition

Snacks and drinks will be served from 8:00-9:00

Hosted by the Friends of Ada Society

5. What is true about the event?

    (A) It aims to honor young women in the arts.
    (B) It is hosted by the family of Ada Lovelace.
    (C) It takes place at the Helmand Events Hall.
    (D) It happens on a different date of the week each year.

6. What will participants most likely see at 7:45 PM?

    (A) two hackers competing
    (B) a bubble and lights show
    (C) a magic show involving numbers
    (D) snack servers offering treats from trays

Part D. General Reading and Retelling

Ada Lovelace, daughter of famous British poet Lord Byron, was born in 1815. From an early age, Lovelace's mother pushed her to study mathematics. Lovelace was often sick as a child, but that did not stop her from continuing her education. In the United Kingdom at the time, girls did not study much math and science in school. Only boys went to those classes. However, Lovelace's mother hired tutors to teach those subjects to her daughter at home. Lovelace had a deep passion for mathematics and studied university-level material on her own. At the age of 17, she met the inventor Charles Babbage. He taught her about his newest invention: the difference engine. This engine could solve math equations automatically when someone put in the numbers. Lovelace saw the potential of this engine, and suggested that it could be used to create automatic programs. Her research and comments on this topic directly led to simple versions of what we would eventually call "computers." During her life, many people did not know of her work, but in the 1950s, the world discovered how much she helped the beginning of development of computer technology. That is why now Ada Lovelace is called the world's "first computer programmer."

7. According to the passage, which of the following best describes Ada Lovelace?

    (A) poet
    (B) biologist
    (C) math tutor
    (D) programmer

8. According to the passage, what is true about Lovelace?

    (A) She studied math and science in a boys' school.
    (B) She majored in mathematics at Oxford University.
    (C) She was the daughter of a famous mathematician.
    (D) She learned math and science from tutors at home.

9. Which of the following would Lovelace most likely say to Babbage?

    (A) "I love all of your poems, Dad."
    (B) "You were my student at university in 1950."
    (C) "I invented something I call the difference engine."
    (D) "Your difference engine could create automatic programs."

10. Which of the following is mentioned in the passage?

    (A) Lovelace never met her own father.
    (B) Lovelace's gambling idea lost a lot of money.
    (C) Lovelace's work was not well known in her lifetime.
    (D) Lovelace translated the work of an Italian mathematician.

Listening Practice

 Listen and write.

  MP3 J3-4

Ada Lovelace

Ada Lovelace, daughter of famous British poet Lord Byron, was born in 1815. From an early age, Lovelace's mother pushed her to study mathematics. Lovelace was often sick as a child, but that did not stop her from continuing her education. In the United Kingdom at the time, girls did not study much math and science in school. Only boys went to those classes. However, Lovelace's mother ¹_____ tutors to teach those ²_____ to her daughter at home. Lovelace had a deep ³_____ for mathematics and studied university-level material on her own. At the age of 17, she met the inventor Charles Babbage. He taught her about his newest ⁴_____: the difference engine. This engine could solve math equations ⁵_____ when someone put in the numbers. Lovelace saw the ⁶_____ of this engine, and suggested that it could be used to create automatic programs. Her research and comments on this topic directly led to simple versions of what we would eventually call "computers." During her life, many people did not know of her work, but in the 1950s, the world discovered how much she helped the beginning of development of computer technology. That is why now Ada Lovelace is called the world's "first computer programmer."

Word Bank

hird	automatic	invenshion
automatically	potential	subjects
invention	hired	passion
subjicts	fashion	potensial

 Listen. Pause. Say each sentence.

  MP3 J3-4G

Writing Practice

  Write the words.

1 _____ X

v ask X to work for you

2 _____

n a topic in school

3 _____

v care a lot about

4 _____

n something new you created

5 _____

adv without humans doing it

6 _____ X

v thought X would later be useful or powerful

Write the words in each blank.

Summary

Ada Lovelace has been called the world's "first _____ programmer." She saw the _____ in an inventor's _____ and suggested that it could be used to create automatic _____.

Word Puzzle

 Complete the word puzzle.

4 ↓
care a lot about

1 ↓
something new you created

3 ↓
ask X to work for you

5 →
thought X would later
be useful or powerful

6 →
a topic in school

2 ↓
without humans doing it

The Edison-Tesla Nobel Prize Rumor

Teacher's Book
p.192

For a while, Nicola Tesla and Thomas Edison were the biggest rivals in the scientific world of electricity. While Tesla hoped to see alternating current (AC) power the world, Edison backed direct current (DC). They sat on opposite sides in this debate. However, Edison and Tesla both had something very big in common: Neither inventor received the Nobel Prize. Moreover, there was even a rumor that both scientists would receive the Nobel Prize in the same year.

In 1915, a newspaper in London reported that both Tesla and Edison were going to receive the Nobel Prize in Physics that year. This story was published in many other newspapers around Europe. However, on November 15, 1915, it was officially announced that the Nobel Prize in Physics would instead go to two scientists who had studied X-rays.

So why was the false rumor published? Some people have said that either Tesla or Edison was going to refuse the Nobel Prize, and that as a result, the judges decided to choose a different recipient. However, the Nobel Prize judges denied this as just a rumor. But this leaves us with a bigger question. Why didn't Tesla or Edison ever receive a Nobel Prize? It is one of the scandals and mysteries in the history of the prize.

CHAPTER 2

Famous People 2

UNIT 5

Tu Youyou

Teacher's Book
p.193

Have you ever heard of Tu Youyou?
Look at the illustration.
What do you think Tu is known for?

Tu Youyou was born in China in 1930 and grew up in a time when scientists there did not receive much respect. In high school, she became very sick with a disease called tuberculosis. Luckily, she recovered and was inspired to study medicine. She first studied traditional Chinese medicine, but eventually her government asked her to find a new cure for malaria, a deadly disease spread by mosquitoes. Using her knowledge of traditional medicine, she and her research team found a plant used in ancient China that might possibly help. However, when they boiled the plant to make the medicine, there was no effect. Tu Youyou was confused but continued her research and found a book from 340 BCE. It said that the plant should not be boiled, but rather soaked in cold water for a long time and then drunk. She tried this process, and it worked! Tu Youyou had found a cure for malaria that has helped millions of people to this day. Her discovery was so important to humanity that Tu won the Nobel Prize for Medicine in 2015, making her the first Chinese woman to receive the honor.

New Words

respect

n honor

recover

v get better after being sick

cure for X

n a treatment for X

boil

v put in very hot water for some time

soak

v leave in water

humanity

n humans

Part A. Sentence Completion

1. A: Is that scientist famous?
   B: Yes! She's so famous _____ she is always surrounded by fans.

   (A) who
   (B) that
   (C) then
   (D) which

2. A: Why did your team do the experiment again?
   B: We were _____ because the first results were completely different from our expectations.

   (A) confuse
   (B) confused
   (C) confuses
   (D) confusing

Part B. Situational Writing

3.

I decided to _____ a potato for dinner.

(A) fry
(B) boil
(C) chop
(D) dice

4.

To get those stains out, _____ the shirt for an hour.

(A) dab
(B) soak
(C) beat
(D) wear

Remember the ABCD Way!

A: Awareness of risk
Find out if you are at risk of getting malaria.

B: Bite prevention
Use insect spray. Put a mosquito net over your bed. Cover your arms and legs with clothing. Use coils.

C: Checking
Do you need to take anti-malaria medication?

D: Diagnosis
Go to the doctor if you think you have symptoms of malaria.

5. Which of the following is the ABCD Way?

(A) names of malaria medications
(B) advice on which countries to visit
(C) approaches to becoming a doctor
(D) tips to avoid the spread of malaria

6. Which of the following is NOT in the list?

(A) sleeping under a net
(B) getting anti-mosquito coils
(C) wearing light colored clothing
(D) talking to a medical professional

Part D. General Reading and Retelling

Tu Youyou was born in China in 1930 and grew up in a time when scientists there did not receive much respect. In high school, she became very sick with a disease called tuberculosis. Luckily, she recovered and was inspired to study medicine. She first studied traditional Chinese medicine, but eventually her government asked her to find a new cure for malaria, a deadly disease spread by mosquitoes. Using her knowledge of traditional medicine, she and her research team found a plant used in ancient China that might possibly help. However, when they boiled the plant to make the medicine, there was no effect. Tu Youyou was confused but continued her research and found a book from 340 BCE. It said that the plant should not be boiled, but rather soaked in cold water for a long time and then drunk. She tried this process, and it worked! Tu Youyou had found a cure for malaria that has helped millions of people to this day. Her discovery was so important to humanity that Tu won the Nobel Prize for Medicine in 2015, making her the first Chinese woman to receive the honor.

7. What is the passage mainly about?

(A) how Tu Youyou overcame tuberculosis
(B) how Tu Youyou found a cure for malaria
(C) why Tu Youyou chose to study medicine
(D) why Tu Youyou invented mosquito spray

8. According to the passage, what did Tu have?

(A) a sister with malaria
(B) an easy job in the government
(C) knowledge of traditional medicine
(D) family members working in hospitals

9. According to the passage, what did Tu learn from a book from 340 BCE?

(A) to plant seeds in spring
(B) to soak a plant in cold water
(C) to boil a plant for a long time
(D) to remove thorns from plants

10. Which fact about Tu is mentioned in the passage?

(A) She studied at Peking University.
(B) She is the Chief Scientist at a famous academy.
(C) She and her team tested 2,000 medicines on mice.
(D) She is the first female Chinese Nobel Prize winner.

Listening Practice

 Listen and write.

  MP3 J3-5

Tu Youyou

Tu Youyou was born in China in 1930 and grew up in a time when scientists there did not receive much ___¹_____ . In high school, she became very sick with a disease called tuberculosis. Luckily, she ²_____ and was inspired to study medicine. She first studied traditional Chinese medicine, but eventually her government asked her to find a new ³_____ malaria, a deadly disease spread by mosquitoes. Using her knowledge of traditional medicine, she and her research team found a plant used in ancient China that might possibly help. However, when they ⁴_____ the plant to make the medicine, there was no effect. Tu Youyou was confused but continued her research and found a book from 340 BCE. It said that the plant should not be boiled, but rather ⁵_____ in cold water for a long time and then drunk. She tried this process, and it worked! Tu Youyou had found a cure for malaria that has helped millions of people to this day. Her discovery was so important to ⁶_____ that Tu won the Nobel Prize for Medicine in 2015, making her the first Chinese woman to receive the honor.

Word Bank

boiled	humenity	humanity
respected	soked	respect
soaked	recobered	boilled
curefor	recovered	cure for

 Listen. Pause. Say each sentence.

  MP3 J3-5G

Writing Practice

 Write the words.

1 _____

n honor

2 _____

v get better after being sick

3 _____ X

n a treatment for X

4 _____

v put in very hot water for some time

5 _____

v leave in water

6 _____

n humans

 Write the words in each blank.

Summary

Chinese Nobel Prize winner Tu Youyou studied traditional Chinese _____.
The government asked her to find a new _____ for malaria, so she and her
_____ team found a _____ that could help, in a discovery that
has been crucial to humans.

Word Puzzle

 Complete the word puzzle.

1 → get better after being sick

1 ↓ honor

2 ↓ leave in water

3 ↓ a treatment for X

4 → humans

5 → put in very hot water for some time

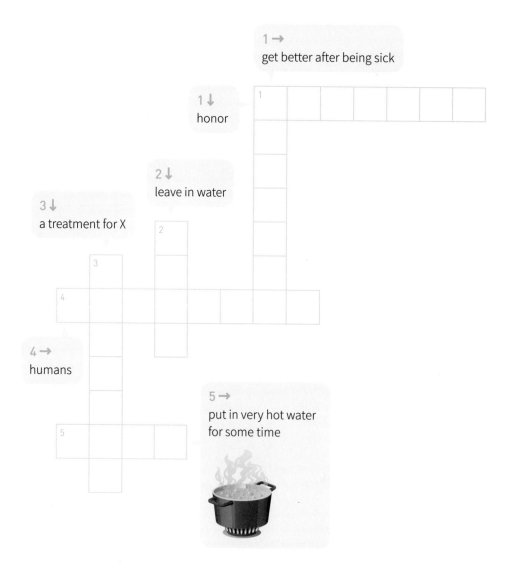

UNIT 6

Teacher's Book p.198

Rigoberta Menchú

Have you ever heard of Rigoberta Menchú?
Look at the illustration.
What do you think Menchú is known for?

Rigoberta Menchú was born in a poor village in Guatemala in 1959. Her country soon fell into a big war that started in 1960. Menchú is part of a group of people called the Maya, and the government was hostile against them. Many people died, but she was able to escape to Mexico. There, she worked hard to save the Mayan people in Guatemala. In 1982, she wrote a book about her experiences living in a poor village and dealing with the war. This book was translated from Spanish into many other languages, making her famous all over the world. Because of her work to help the Maya and other people in her country, she received the Nobel Peace Prize in 1992. She used her prize money to start the Rigoberta Menchú Tum Foundation to protect the rights of the Maya. The long war in Guatemala finally ended in 1996. Since then, Menchú's book has been criticized, as some of the events in it did not happen. Still, Menchú continues to be a representative for many Mayan people and even ran for President of Guatemala twice! Her life proves that even someone born in a small village can have a giant impact on her country and the entire world.

New Words

hostile
adj not friendly

escape
v get away

protect
v keep safe

rights
n laws protecting people

representative for X
n a person who speaks for X

have an impact on
v affect

Part A. Sentence Completion

1. A: What happened that year?
    B: Many people _____ in the war, and many others were injured.

    (A) died
    (B) had dead
    (C) were died
    (D) have been dead

2. A: Did you enjoy this book?
    B: Yes, it was great. It was translated from Chinese _____ English.

    (A) for
    (B) into
    (C) beside
    (D) against

Part B. Situational Writing

3.
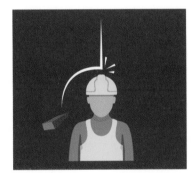

Wear this to _____ your head.

(A) soften
(B) lighten
(C) protect
(D) highlight

4.

This dog is quite _____.

(A) timid
(B) hostile
(C) friendly
(D) bubbly

Guatemala

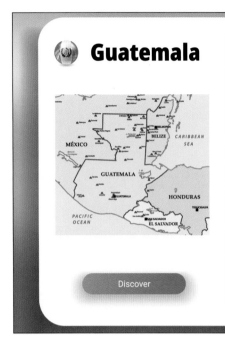

Official name: Republic of Gatemala
Population: 17 million people   **Currency:** Quetzal
Total area: 108,890 km²   **Capital:** Guatemala City
Official language: Spanish / 23 other languages
(officially recognized, including Mayan ones)
Ethnic groups: 41% Mestizo / 40% Maya / 18% European / 1% Other

National birds:

Quetzal

Famous industry:

Mayan
Weaving

Famous sites:

Tikal
Ancient Mayan Ruins,
UNESCO World Heritage Site

Antigua
UNESCO World Heritage Site

Discover

5. According to the chart, which of the following is true about Guatemala?

(A) There are 23 official languages.
(B) It separated Honduras and El Salvador.
(C) Over 60% of its population is Mayan people.
(D) Its money and national bird share the same name.

6. Which of the following would a tourist in Antigua most likely say?

(A) "It is beautiful here in Guatemala's modern capital!"
(B) "I can understand why UNESCO chose this place!"
(C) "This place's most famous export is ski equipment!"
(D) "I can't believe 17 million people live in this one city!"

Rigoberta Menchú was born in a poor village in Guatemala in 1959. Her country soon fell into a big war that started in 1960. Menchú is part of a group of people called the Maya, and the government was hostile against them. Many people died, but she was able to escape to Mexico. There, she worked hard to save the Mayan people in Guatemala. In 1982, she wrote a book about her experiences living in a poor village and dealing with the war. This book was translated from Spanish into many other languages, making her famous all over the world. Because of her work to help the Maya and other people in her country, she received the Nobel Peace Prize in 1992. She used her prize money to start the Rigoberta Menchú Tum Foundation to protect the rights of the Maya. The long war in Guatemala finally ended in 1996. Since then, Menchú's book has been criticized, as some of the events in it did not happen. Still, Menchú continues to be a representative for many Mayan people and even ran for President of Guatemala twice! Her life proves that even someone born in a small village can have a giant impact on her country and the entire world.

7. Which would be the best title for the passage?

   (A) Why a Mexican Doctor Won a Battle
   (B) Spanish Doctor, President of Guatemala
   (C) Mayan Woman, Nobel Peace Prize Winner
   (D) How a Nurse from Guatemala Won the Nobel Prize

8. According to the passage, why did Menchú most likely go to Mexico?

   (A) to marry someone living in Mexico City
   (B) to escape the government of Guatemala
   (C) to study whales who came to Mexican water
   (D) to visit a cousin who lived by a famous beach

9. According to the passage, what did Menchú write?

   (A) a textbook for soldiers
   (B) a poem about life in Mexico
   (C) a book about village life and war
   (D) a manual to train nurses and doctors

10. Which of the following is NOT mentioned in the passage?

   (A) The war in Guatemala lasted for 36 years.
   (B) Menchú received the Nobel Peace Prize in 1992.
   (C) Menchú started a foundation with her prize money.
   (D) The Guatemalan president thanked Menchú personally.

Listening Practice

 Listen and write.

  MP3 J3-6

Rigoberta Menchú

Rigoberta Menchú was born in a poor village in Guatemala in 1959. Her country soon fell into a big war that started in 1960. Menchú is part of a group of people called the Maya, and the government was ¹ _____ against them. Many people died, but she was able to ² _____ to Mexico. There, she worked hard to save the Mayan people in Guatemala. In 1982, she wrote a book about her experiences living in a poor village and dealing with the war. This book was translated from Spanish into many other languages, making her famous all over the world. Because of her work to help the Maya and other people in her country, she received the Nobel Peace Prize in 1992. She used her prize money to start the Rigoberta Menchú Tum Foundation to ³ _____ the ⁴ _____ of the Maya. The long war in Guatemala finally ended in 1996. Since then, Menchú's book has been criticized, as some of the events in it did not happen. Still, Menchú continues to be a ⁵ _____ for many Mayan people and even ran for President of Guatemala twice! Her life proves that even someone born in a small village can have a giant ⁶ _____ on her country and the entire world.

Word Bank

hostile	impect	escape
escaype	writes	hostil
representative	protect	protected
representetive	impact	rights

 Listen. Pause. Say each sentence.

  MP3 J3-6G

Writing Practice

 Write the words.

1 _____

adj not friendly

2 _____

v get away

3 _____

v keep safe

4 _____

n laws protecting people

5 _____ X

n a person who speaks for X

6 _____

v affect

 Write the words in each blank.

Summary

Nobel Peace Prize Winner Rigoberta Menchú worked to _____ the Maya and other people in the country of _____ when they were suffering from poverty and _____. She still has a giant _____ on her country and the entire world.

Word Puzzle

 Complete the word puzzle.

1 ↓ laws protecting people

2 ↓ keep safe

3 ↓ a person who speaks for X

4 → not friendly

5 → get away

6 → affect

UNIT 7

Antoni Gaudi

Teacher's Book p.204

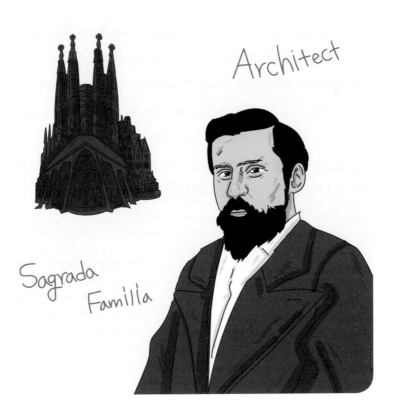

Have you ever heard of Antoni Gaudi?
Look at the illustration.
What do you think Gaudi was known for?

There are well-known architects from all over the world. However, one of the most famous of all is Antoni Gaudi. A very creative architect from Barcelona, Spain, Gaudi made many special buildings. One of his most famous buildings, La Sagrada Familia, is a giant Catholic church. Interestingly, Gaudi started building La Sagrada Familia in 1882, but the church is still not finished! Gaudi left plans for future architects to finish it. Another place designed by Gaudi is Park Güell. The original plan was for a set of buildings for a man named Güell. Güell hired Gaudi to make the buildings. But Güell did not have enough money to finish them. Therefore, they became a park later on. Another famous Gaudi building is Casa Milà (also called "La Pedrera"). Casa Milà was the last house Gaudi built, and it was finished in 1906. It has an interesting look because the walls curve. The outside walls are made from more than 6,000 blocks of stone joined with metal. But they do not look like plain blocks. Instead, they look like curvy waves. It is an unusual building to be downtown in a city. In 1984, UNESCO made it a special world site. These three unique places all show Gaudi's creativity as an architect.

New Words

plans

n drawings of a building

original

adj first

later on

adv after some time

curve

v do not go in a straight line

unusual

adj not common

unique

adj different from everything else

Part A. Sentence Completion

1. A: I started _____ this table last year.
   B: When will it be finished?

   (A) make
   (B) maker
   (C) making
   (D) to making

2. A: Why is that architect in the news these days?
   B: He has designed _____ building.

   (A) other
   (B) another
   (C) other his
   (D) another his

Part B. Situational Writing

3. 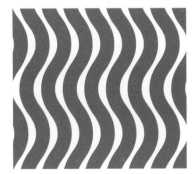 He puts a lot of _____ lines in his art.

   (A) black
   (B) curvy
   (C) dotted
   (D) straight

4. 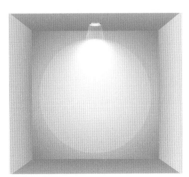 The walls in the room are _____.

   (A) plain
   (B) bumpy
   (C) decorated
   (D) tangerine

Park Güell Tour

90-minute private tours with a knowledgeable and certified guide.

❖ Learn about the history of Gaudi's Park Güell!

❖ See details of the architecture—including the famous Dragon Stairway.

Other benefits: Skip the line—go directly into the park with your guide.

Tours of 2 to 5 people	Booking available up to 48 hours in advance	Cost: 10 euro per person Free for children 5 and under

5. Which of the following is NOT mentioned about the tour?

(A) the price of the tour

(B) how long the tour lasts

(C) where to meet the guide

(D) the minimum number of people allowed

6. The Kim family wants to take a tour on Friday, April 10, 10 AM. When is their deadline to book it?

(A) Wednesday, April 8, 10 AM

(B) Thursday, April 9, 12 noon

(C) Friday, April 10, 8 AM

(D) Friday, April 10, 9 AM

Part D. General Reading and Retelling

There are well-known architects from all over the world. However, one of the most famous of all is Antoni Gaudi. A very creative architect from Barcelona, Spain, Gaudi made many special buildings. One of his most famous buildings, La Sagrada Familia, is a giant Catholic church. Interestingly, Gaudi started building La Sagrada Familia in 1882, but the church is still not finished! Gaudi left plans for future architects to finish it. Another place designed by Gaudi is Park Güell. The original plan was for a set of buildings for a man named Güell. Güell hired Gaudi to make the buildings. But Güell did not have enough money to finish them. Therefore, they became a park later on. Another famous Gaudi building is Casa Milà (also called "La Pedrera"). Casa Milà was the last house Gaudi built, and it was finished in 1906. It has an interesting look because the walls curve. The outside walls are made from more than 6,000 blocks of stone joined with metal. But they do not look like plain blocks. Instead, they look like curvy waves. It is an unusual building to be downtown in a city. In 1984, UNESCO made it a special world site. These three unique places all show Gaudi's creativity as an architect.

7. What is the main idea of the passage?

  (A) Gaudi's buildings curve.
  (B) Barcelona is a pretty city.
  (C) Spain has beautiful buildings.
  (D) Gaudi made special buildings.

8. According to the passage, what is NOT true about La Sagrada Familia?

  (A) It is a Catholic church.
  (B) It was Gaudi's last building.
  (C) Future architects will finish it.
  (D) Gaudi started building it in 1882.

9. According to the passage, how did Park Güell get its name?

  (A) Güell paid Gaudi to build it.
  (B) Güell was Gaudi's best friend.
  (C) Güell died while building the park.
  (D) Güell was the city Gaudi was born in.

10. Which place is also called La Pedrera?

  (A) Barcelona
  (B) Casa Milà
  (C) Park Güell
  (D) La Sagrada Familia

Listening Practice

 Listen and write.

  MP3 J3-7

Antoni Gaudi

There are well-known architects from all over the world. However, one of the most famous of all is Antoni Gaudi. A very creative architect from Barcelona, Spain, Gaudi made many special buildings. One of his most famous buildings, La Sagrada Familia, is a giant Catholic church. Interestingly, Gaudi started building La Sagrada Familia in 1882, but the church is still not finished! Gaudi left ¹ _____ for future architects to finish it. Another place designed by Gaudi is Park Güell. The ² _____ plan was for a set of buildings for a man named Güell. Güell hired Gaudi to make the buildings. But Güell did not have enough money to finish them. Therefore, they became a park ³ _____. Another famous Gaudi building is Casa Milà (also called "La Pedrera"). Casa Milà was the last house Gaudi built, and it was finished in 1906. It has an interesting look because the walls ⁴ _____. The outside walls are made from more than 6,000 blocks of stone joined with metal. But they do not look like plain blocks. Instead, they look like curvy waves. It is an ⁵ _____ building to be downtown in a city. In 1984, UNESCO made it a special world site. These three ⁶ _____ places all show Gaudi's creativity as an architect.

Word Bank

curb	later on	unusuel
younique	orginel	flans
plans	original	unusual
curve	late her on	unique

 Listen. Pause. Say each sentence.

  MP3 J3-7G

Writing Practice

 Write the words.

1 _____

n drawings of a building

2 _____

adj first

3 _____

adv after some time

4 _____

v do not go in a straight line

5 _____

adj not common

6 _____

adj different from everything else

 Write the words in each blank.

Summary

Antoni Gaudi is one of the most famous _____ in the world. He made many special _____ such as La Sagrada Familia, Park Güell, and Casa Milà. These three _____ places all show Gaudi's _____ as an architect.

Word Puzzle

 Complete the word puzzle.

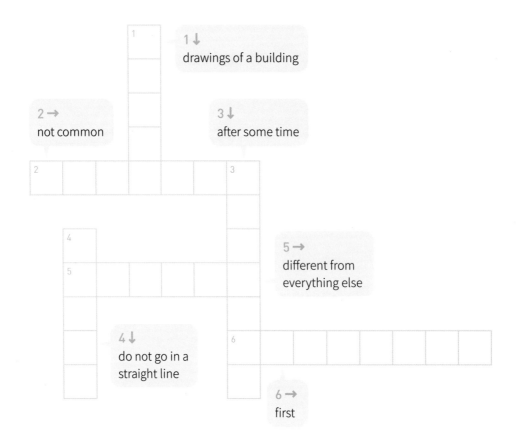

1 ↓ drawings of a building

2 → not common

3 ↓ after some time

5 → different from everything else

4 ↓ do not go in a straight line

6 → first

UNIT 8

Wangari Maathai

Teacher's Book p.209

Have you ever heard of Wangari Maathai?
Look at the illustration.
What do you think Maathai was known for?

Wangari Maathai was a respected scientist, politician, and environmental activist. She had college degrees in biology and science for veterinarians. A Kenyan, Maathai was also the first black African woman to receive a Nobel Prize. She led a lot of very important projects. These projects helped the environment and women. However, one of her most famous projects was related to trees. She founded something called the Green Belt Movement. Her idea was that women in villages could help create a source of fuel and at the same time stop deserts from spreading. To achieve this, Maathai said that women could plant trees. The organization began in 1977. By the year 2000, the Green Belt Movement had planted almost 30 million trees. Moreover, thanks to Maathai's leadership, people in other countries, including Tanzania, Ethiopia, and Zimbabwe, started similar projects with trees. Maathai famously said, "When we plant trees, we plant the seeds of hope." Along with hope, the Green Belt Movement has brought stronger soil, better ways of storing rainwater, firewood, food, and money. Maathai died in 2011. But her incredible story is a reminder of how much one person can influence others and begin long-lasting changes in the world.

New Words

activist	**veterinarian**
n a person who tries to get social changes to happen	*n* a person who helps sick animals
found	**thanks to**
v start an organization	*prep* because of
soil	**influence others**
n dirt for growing plants	*v* make others change

Part A. Sentence Completion

1. A: The earth is getting warmer. Can we stop that?
    B: Maybe we can prevent the problem _____ getting worse.

    (A) in
    (B) on
    (C) as
    (D) from

2. A: What has your charity program done this year?
    B: We have _____ books to kids in poor countries.

    (A) bring
    (B) brang
    (C) bringed
    (D) brought

Part B. Situational Writing

3.

My uncle is a _____.

(A) chemist
(B) landscaper
(C) pharmacist
(D) veterinarian

4.

She is _____ by her teammates.

(A) taught
(B) disliked
(C) annoyed
(D) respected

The Great Green Wall

- Goal: 8,000km natural wonder that crosses the entire width of Africa, near the Sahara Desert

- Starting date: 2007

- Will be the world's largest living structure when it is finished (3 times as big as Australia's Great Barrier Reef)

- 15% finished at present

- Hope: Heal ruined landscapes, secure food, create jobs

5. According to the information, what is true about the Great Green Wall?

    (A) It was first begun in 2009.
    (B) It is currently 15% complete.
    (C) It was founded by Wangari Maathai.
    (D) It is the same size as the Great Barrier Reef.

6. Which is specifically listed as a hope for the Great Green Wall?

    (A) creating a wind farm
    (B) connecting Asia and Africa
    (C) bringing tourists to the Sahara
    (D) aiding in making jobs for people

Part D. General Reading and Retelling

Wangari Maathai was a respected scientist, politician, and environmental activist. She had college degrees in biology and science for veterinarians. A Kenyan, Maathai was also the first black African woman to receive a Nobel Prize. She led a lot of very important projects. These projects helped the environment and women. However, one of her most famous projects was related to trees. She founded something called the Green Belt Movement. Her idea was that women in villages could help create a source of fuel and at the same time stop deserts from spreading. To achieve this, Maathai said that women could plant trees. The organization began in 1977. By the year 2000, the Green Belt Movement had planted almost 30 million trees. Moreover, thanks to Maathai's leadership, people in other countries, including Tanzania, Ethiopia, and Zimbabwe, started similar projects with trees. Maathai famously said, "When we plant trees, we plant the seeds of hope." Along with hope, the Green Belt Movement has brought stronger soil, better ways of storing rainwater, firewood, food, and money. Maathai died in 2011. But her incredible story is a reminder of how much one person can influence others and begin long-lasting changes in the world.

7. What is the passage mainly about?

(A) Wangari Maathai's childhood
(B) Wangari Maathai's studies in college
(C) Wangari Maathai's influence after death
(D) Wangari Maathai's Green Belt Movement

8. What country did Maathai come from?

(A) Kenya
(B) Ethiopia
(C) Tanzania
(D) Zimbabwe

9. What Green Belt Movement effect is NOT mentioned in the passage?

(A) getting stronger soil
(B) saving animal homes
(C) creating a fuel source
(D) improving rainwater storage

10. Which is most similar to Maathai's quote in the passage?

(A) Pine trees are strong.
(B) Trees can bring hope.
(C) Each tree has secrets.
(D) Money does not grow on trees.

Listening Practice

 Listen and write.

  MP3 J3-8

Wangari Maathai

Wangari Maathai was a respected scientist, politician, and environmental

1 _____ . She had college degrees in biology and science for

2 _____ . A Kenyan, Maathai was also the first black African woman to receive a Nobel Prize. She led a lot of very important projects. These projects helped the environment and women. However, one of her most famous projects was related to trees. She 3 _____ something called the Green Belt Movement. Her idea was that women in villages could help create a source of fuel and at the same time stop deserts from spreading. To achieve this, Maathai said that women could plant trees. The organization began in 1977. By the year 2000, the Green Belt Movement had planted almost 30 million trees. Moreover, 4 _____ to Maathai's leadership, people in other countries, including Tanzania, Ethiopia, and Zimbabwe, started similar projects with trees. Maathai famously said, "When we plant trees, we plant the seeds of hope."

Along with hope, the Green Belt Movement has brought stronger 5 _____ , better ways of storing rainwater, firewood, food, and money. Maathai died in 2011. But her incredible story is a reminder of how much one person can 6 _____ others and begin long-lasting changes in the world.

Word Bank

beterinarians	soil	activist
founded	found	activists
influence	thank	soyl
thanks	veterinarians	inpluence

 Listen. Pause. Say each sentence.

  MP3 J3-8G

Writing Practice

 Write the words.

1 _____

n a person who tries to get social changes to happen

2 _____

n a person who helps sick animals

3 _____

v start an organization

4 _____

prep because of

5 _____

n dirt for growing plants

6 _____

v make others change

 Write the words in each blank.

Summary

Among the many projects Nobel Prize winner Wangari Maathai did to save the

_____, the Green _____ Movement is the most famous. She

has had an incredible _____ in getting people to plant _____.

Word Puzzle

 Complete the word puzzle.

1 →
a person who tries to get social changes to happen

2 ↓
because of

3 →
a person who helps sick animals

4 ↓
make others change

5 →
start an organization

6 →
dirt for growing plants

Foreign Accent Syndrome

 Teacher's Book p.215

Winners of the Nobel Prize in Medicine have helped the world with all kinds of medical problems. However, there are still many unsolved mysteries about health and the human body. One of these mysteries is foreign accent syndrome.

People suffering from foreign accent syndrome tend to have had head injuries. Sometimes sufferers get hit in the head and then wake up. When they wake up, suddenly they sound like they are speaking with a foreign accent. In one case, a woman from Norway started to sound like she had German accent. In another, a native English-speaking man from the UK sounded like a native Spanish speaker.

In the past, doctors thought that the condition was psychological. However, new technology has helped medical scientists to learn more about the brain. Now it is thought that damage to a certain part of the brain causes foreign accent syndrome.

What is not certain, though, is why some people with foreign accent syndrome can use an accent they have never heard before. Medical scientists think this has to do with listeners. In fact, people suffering from foreign accent syndrome do not speak a new language. They just have trouble making some sounds. It seems that listeners hear sufferers and think they sound like they have a foreign accent. However, no one knows for sure what is happening in foreign accent syndrome. It is one of life's many medical mysteries.

CHAPTER 3

Famous People 3

UNIT 9

Mary Jackson

Teacher's Book
p.216

NASA's First Black Female Engineer

Have you ever heard of Mary Jackson?
Look at the illustration.
What do you think Jackson was known for?

Mary Jackson was an engineer and mathematician who worked at NASA. She was born in 1921. Where she lived at that time, black people were not allowed to go to school with white people. The schools for black people were often bad in quality, so she had to study extra hard to receive a good education. After university, she started working as a "computer" — someone who solved difficult math problems on Earth when rockets were sent into space. Jackson worked on a team called the "West Area Computers." They were a group of black women who used data to decide the best way for spaceships to fly. Eventually, Mary Jackson trained to become an engineer. This made her the first black woman to become an engineer at NASA. She was an intelligent and hard worker, but her bosses would not make her a manager. Many people thought only white men could become managers. Jackson decided to change her job and became the head of NASA's women's program. There, she worked to give women more opportunities in all parts of the space program. Thanks to Mary Jackson and others like her, now anyone can work at any job in NASA if they have the right skills and work hard.

New Words

bad in quality *adj* ineffective	**spaceship** *n* a vehicle for people to travel into space
eventually *adv* finally after trying for a long time	**train to** *v* go to classes to learn how to
head of *n* leader of	**opportunity** *n* chance

Part A. Sentence Completion

1. A: What does your sister do?

    B: She is training _____ a software engineer.

    (A) became
    (B) to become
    (C) be become
    (D) will become

2. A: What is _____ way to get into that program?

    B: Study extra hard and do lots of volunteer work.

    (A) best
    (B) the best
    (C) the most good
    (D) the most better

Part B. Situational Writing

3.

Jan

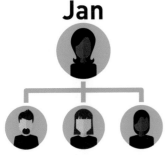

Jan is the _____ of our department.

(A) head

(B) lowest

(C) funniest

(D) assistant

4.

There is going to be a _____ launch tonight.

(A) satellite

(B) building

(C) basement

(D) spaceship

UNIT 9 Mary Jackson

Bored over winter break?
Have an adventure at the Robot and Space Academy!
Work with kind (human) counselors!

What you will do:

1) Program robots
2) Simulate a space mission
3) Use data and math to plan a mock space flight to Mars!

Who can join: Any science-lover attending middle or high school

Orientation: 1:30 PM, February 1
Graduation ceremony: February 8
Optional: Overnight stays
            (see here for additional prices)

Total cost:

450,000 KRW
per attendee

5. For whom is the ad most likely written?

(A) a former astronaut who wants to teach
(B) a high schooler interested in the planets
(C) a preschooler who wants to build robots
(D) a college student who studies astronomy

6. What is true about the academy?

(A) The counselors are robots.
(B) The academy lasts one week.
(C) The attendees must stay overnight.
(D) The workshops occur during summer.

Mary Jackson was an engineer and mathematician who worked at NASA. She was born in 1921. Where she lived at that time, black people were not allowed to go to school with white people. The schools for black people were often bad in quality, so she had to study extra hard to receive a good education. After university, she started working as a "computer" — someone who solved difficult math problems on Earth when rockets were sent into space. Jackson worked on a team called the "West Area Computers." They were a group of black women who used data to decide the best way for spaceships to fly. Eventually, Mary Jackson trained to become an engineer. This made her the first black woman to become an engineer at NASA. She was an intelligent and hard worker, but her bosses would not make her a manager. Many people thought only white men could become managers. Jackson decided to change her job and became the head of NASA's women's program. There, she worked to give women more opportunities in all parts of the space program. Thanks to Mary Jackson and others like her, now anyone can work at any job in NASA if they have the right skills and work hard.

7. According to the passage, which of the following is true?

   (A) Mary Jackson founded NASA.
   (B) Mary Jackson went into outer space.
   (C) Mary Jackson was born in the 1920s.
   (D) Mary Jackson went to an all-white school.

8. According to the passage, why did Jackson study extra hard for a good education?

   (A) Her parents were extremely strict.
   (B) Her regular school was low in quality.
   (C) She was very sick when she was a child.
   (D) She started school later than most children.

9. What did the West Area Computers do?

   (A) invent talking robots
   (B) use data to help spaceships fly
   (C) hire white women as programmers
   (D) join metal spaceship parts together

10. Which of the following is most likely true?

   (A) Jackson disliked science.
   (B) Jackson walked on the moon.
   (C) Jackson helped women of any race.
   (D) Jackson banned NASA's women's program.

UNIT 9　Mary Jackson

Listen and write.

  MP3 J3-9

Mary Jackson

Mary Jackson was an engineer and mathematician who worked at NASA. She was born in 1921. Where she lived at that time, black people were not allowed to go to school with white people. The schools for black people were often bad in ¹ _____ , so she had to study extra hard to receive a good education. After university, she started working as a "computer" — someone who solved difficult math problems on Earth when rockets were sent into space. Jackson worked on a team called the "West Area Computers." They were a group of black women who used data to decide the best way for ² _____ to fly. ³ _____ , Mary Jackson ⁴ _____ to become an engineer. This made her the first black woman to become an engineer at NASA. She was an intelligent and hard worker, but her bosses would not make her a manager. Many people thought only white men could become managers. Jackson decided to change her job and became the ⁵ _____ NASA's women's program. There, she worked to give women more ⁶ _____ in all parts of the space program. Thanks to Mary Jackson and others like her, now anyone can work at any job in NASA if they have the right skills and work hard.

Word Bank

trained	spaceships	head of
quality	traned	Eventually
oportunities	spacesips	opportunities
eventually	headuv	qality

 Listen. Pause. Say each sentence.

  MP3 J3-9G

Writing Practice

 Write the words.

1 _____

adj ineffective

2 _____

n a vehicle for people to travel into space

3 _____

adv finally after trying for a long time

4 _____

v go to classes to learn how to

5 _____

n leader of

6 _____

n chance

 Write the words in each blank.

Summary

Mary Jackson was the first black _____ to become an engineer at NASA. She became the _____ of NASA's women's program. Then, she worked hard to give women more _____ in all parts of the _____ program.

Word Puzzle

Complete the word puzzle.

1 ↓
chance

2 →
a vehicle for people to travel into space

3 ↓
ineffective

4 ↓
go to classes to learn how to

5 ↓
leader of

6 →
finally after trying for a long time

UNIT 10

Isabel Allende

Teacher's Book p.221

Have you ever heard of Isabel Allende?
Look at the illustration.
What do you think Allende is known for?

Isabel Allende was born in 1942. Her family was very powerful in the government of Chile, and her cousin Salvador Allende was even president! However, some Chileans did not like Salvador Allende, especially some generals in the military. They took over the government in 1973, and Isabel Allende escaped from Chile to Venezuela so she would not be put in prison or killed. In 1981, she heard that her 99-year-old grandfather was sick. She began writing a letter to him. The letter became so long that she turned it into a book called *The House of Spirits*. The book is based on her life and the life of her family living in Chile. Allende mixed in elements of magic and fantasy as part of a genre called *magical realism*. *The House of Spirits* was a bestseller immediately and has been translated into almost 40 different languages. Because of this and other works, Isabel Allende has received many awards, including the National Prize for Literature in Chile and the Presidential Medal of Freedom in the United States. She even held a flag in the opening ceremony of the 2006 Turin Winter Olympics. These honors, along with worldwide book sales, make her one of the most famous female Latin American authors ever.

New Words

general

n someone in a high position in the military

take over

v get control of

be based on

v be about

bestseller

n a very popular book

translate

v change from one language to another

worldwide

adj all over the world

Part A. Sentence Completion

1. A: Was this book first written in Vietnamese?
    B: Yes. But then it was translated _____ English.

    (A) for
    (B) into
    (C) from
    (D) under

2. A: I love this author.
    B: Me, too. She has received _____ awards for her great writing.

    (A) bit
    (B) least
    (C) each
    (D) many

Part B. Situational Writing

3.

This song is popular _____.

(A) yearly
(B) worldwide
(C) for holidays
(D) under water

4.

The man is trying to _____ the crocodile.

(A) feed
(B) trap
(C) run toward
(D) escape from

Movie Reviews

The House of the Spirits

Reviewer: Chen Jianguo

Who would imagine that such an exciting book as *The House of the Spirits* could become such an awful movie? Were the actors talented? Sure, but not a single one of them was from Latin America. Were the sets beautiful? Yes, but they were not realistic. Yet, somehow this movie transformed the book's colorful melodrama into something very dull.

Reviewer: Makiko Fujimoto

I know that many critics did not love this movie, but I thought it was okay. It features a great cast of actors, beautiful costumes, and impressive sets. It would have been good if the movie were closer to the original novel (which was better than the film). However, it was still quite good.

5. What is true about both reviewers?

   (A) They strongly disliked a book.
   (B) They strongly disliked a movie
   (C) They liked a movie better than a book.
   (D) They liked a book better than a movie.

6. What change to the movie would Chen Jianguo most likely want?

   (A) beautiful sets
   (B) less melodrama
   (C) fewer bright colors
   (D) Latin American actors

Part D. General Reading and Retelling

Isabel Allende was born in 1942. Her family was very powerful in the government of Chile, and her cousin Salvador Allende was even president! However, some Chileans did not like Salvador Allende, especially some generals in the military. They took over the government in 1973, and Isabel Allende escaped from Chile to Venezuela so she would not be put in prison or killed. In 1981, she heard that her 99-year-old grandfather was sick. She began writing a letter to him. The letter became so long that she turned it into a book called *The House of Spirits*. The book is based on her life and the life of her family living in Chile. Allende mixed in elements of magic and fantasy as part of a genre called *magical realism*. *The House of Spirits* was a bestseller immediately and has been translated into almost 40 different languages. Because of this and other works, Isabel Allende has received many awards, including the National Prize for Literature in Chile and the Presidential Medal of Freedom in the United States. She even held a flag in the opening ceremony of the 2006 Turin Winter Olympics. These honors, along with worldwide book sales, make her one of the most famous female Latin American authors ever.

7. Which would be the best title for the passage?

    (A) The Oldest Writer in Venezuela
    (B) The President of Chile Writes a Book
    (C) A Prize-winning Author from Latin America
    (D) An International Lawyer and Part-time Magician

8. According to the passage, what happened in Chile in 1973?

    (A) Isabel Allende was put in prison.
    (B) Isabel Allende was elected president.
    (C) Military generals took over the government.
    (D) Military soldiers helped the Allendes get back into Chile.

9. How did Isabel Allende start writing *The House of Spirits*?

    (A) by meeting a magician
    (B) as a letter to her grandfather
    (C) by attending a language class
    (D) as a traditional song from Chile

10. What did Isabel Allende do at the 2006 Olympics?

    (A) win a race
    (B) hold a flag
    (C) give a speech
    (D) travel to Japan

Listening Practice

 Listen and write.

  MP3 J3-10

Isabel Allende

Isabel Allende was born in 1942. Her family was very powerful in the government of Chile, and her cousin Salvador Allende was even president! However, some Chileans did not like Salvador Allende, especially some ¹_____ in the military. They ²_____ the government in 1973, and Isabel Allende escaped from Chile to Venezuela so she would not be put in prison or killed. In 1981, she heard that her 99-year-old grandfather was sick. She began writing a letter to him. The letter became so long that she turned it into a book called *The House of Spirits*. The book is ³_____ on her life and the life of her family living in Chile. Allende mixed in elements of magic and fantasy as part of a genre called *magical realism*. *The House of Spirits* was a ⁴_____ immediately and has been ⁵_____ into almost 40 different languages. Because of this and other works, Isabel Allende has received many awards, including the National Prize for Literature in Chile and the Presidential Medal of Freedom in the United States. She even held a flag in the opening ceremony of the 2006 Turin Winter Olympics. These honors, along with ⁶_____ book sales, make her one of the most famous female Latin American authors ever.

Word Bank

bestseller	base	took off her
wordwide	based	worldwide
generals	took over	bestsaller
transladed	jenerals	translated

 Listen. Pause. Say each sentence.

  MP3 J3-10G

Writing Practice

 Write the words.

1 _____

n someone in a high position in the military

2 _____

v get control of

3 _____

v be about

4 _____

n a very popular book

5 _____

v change from one language to another

6 _____

adj all over the world

 Write the words in each blank.

Summary

Isabel Allende is one of the most famous female Latin American _____.

Her prize-winning _____, *The House of Spirits*, has been _____

into many _____.

Word Puzzle

  Complete the word puzzle.

1 ↓ be about

2 ↓ a very popular book

3 ↓ all over the world

4 ↓ someone in a high position in the military

5 → change from one language to another

6 → get control of

UNIT 11

Pius Mau Piailug

Teacher's Book p.227

Have you ever heard of Pius "Mau" Piailug?
Look at the illustration.
What do you think Mau was known for?

Pius "Mau" Piailug was born in 1932 on Satawal, a small island in the nation of Micronesia. He learned traditional methods for sailing that were used before GPS and maps. Instead, Mau looked at the stars, clouds, winds, water movements, and even animals to know his location and his direction. By the age of 18, he had become a "palu," a master in traditional sailing techniques. As Mau grew older, the lifestyle of his people on Satawal began to change. Young people were going to newly-built schools to learn Western subjects, and traditional life began to disappear and be forgotten. This made Mau worried. In order to prove the value of traditional sailing techniques, he teamed up with some researchers to sail from Hawaii to Tahiti using only the knowledge he received in his village. No modern technology would be used. The trip took 34 days, but it was successful. This proved that ancient people could travel long distances without maps or computers. In addition, interest in traditional Micronesian and Polynesian culture increased after the trip. Mau's efforts helped save knowledge from many centuries from disappearing forever, and people still celebrate his efforts today.

New Words

sailing
n   moving in a boat on water

prove
v   show for sure

increase
v   go up

ancient
adj   from a long time ago

long distance
n   a long space

interest in X
n   caring about X

ex   When people have an interest in X, they care about X.

Part A. Sentence Completion

1. A: Why is he called a master?
    B: He knows a lot of impressive traditional _____.

    (A) technique
    (B) techniques
    (C) a technique
    (D) his technique

2. A: Was your grandmother always good at art?
    B: Yes. By the age of ten, she _____ a painting.

    (A) already sells
    (B) already selling
    (C) has already sell
    (D) had already sold

Part B. Situational Writing

3.

They are _____ by the islands.

    (A) sailing
    (B) rowing
    (C) running
    (D) swimming

4.

Last year, prices _____.

    (A) fell
    (B) stabilized
    (C) increased
    (D) decreased

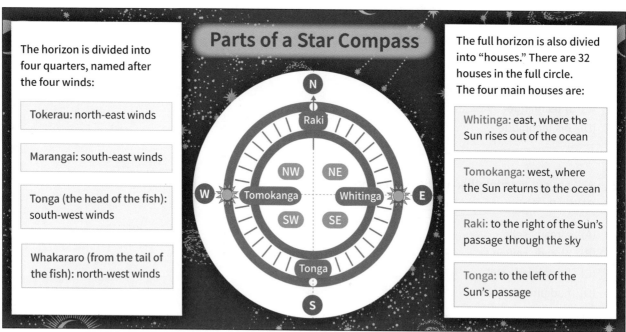

The horizon is divided into four quarters, named after the four winds:

Tokerau: north-east winds

Marangai: south-east winds

Tonga (the head of the fish): south-west winds

Whakararo (from the tail of the fish): north-west winds

Parts of a Star Compass

The full horizon is also divied into "houses." There are 32 houses in the full circle.
The four main houses are:

Whitinga: east, where the Sun rises out of the ocean

Tomokanga: west, where the Sun returns to the ocean

Raki: to the right of the Sun's passage through the sky

Tonga: to the left of the Sun's passage

5. If the star compass included labels for major winds, where would the "head of the fish" be located?

   (A) top left

   (B) top right

   (C) bottom left

   (D) bottom right

6. From which house does the Sun rise?

   (A) Whitinga

   (B) Tomokanga

   (C) Raki

   (D) Tonga

Part D. General Reading and Retelling

Pius "Mau" Piailug was born in 1932 on Satawal, a small island in the nation of Micronesia. He learned traditional methods for sailing that were used before GPS and maps. Instead, Mau looked at the stars, clouds, winds, water movements, and even animals to know his location and his direction. By the age of 18, he had become a "palu," a master in traditional sailing techniques. As Mau grew older, the lifestyle of his people on Satawal began to change. Young people were going to newly-built schools to learn Western subjects, and traditional life began to disappear and be forgotten. This made Mau worried. In order to prove the value of traditional sailing techniques, he teamed up with some researchers to sail from Hawaii to Tahiti using only the knowledge he received in his village. No modern technology would be used. The trip took 34 days, but it was successful. This proved that ancient people could travel long distances without maps or computers. In addition, interest in traditional Micronesian and Polynesian culture increased after the trip. Mau's efforts helped save knowledge from many centuries from disappearing forever, and people still celebrate his efforts today.

7. Which of Mau's worries is mentioned in the passage?

(A) global warming
(B) oceans becoming polluted
(C) traditional life being forgotten
(D) islands sinking into the ocean

8. According to the passage, which of the following did Mau use to find his direction?

(A) radios
(B) clouds
(C) paper maps
(D) smoke signals

9. According to the passage, how long was Mau's journey?

(A) a week
(B) half a month
(C) just over a month
(D) two months

10. What does the underlined "Mau's efforts" most likely mean?

(A) Mau helped animals be free.
(B) Mau spoke several languages.
(C) Mau helped save ancient knowledge.
(D) Mau brought Western subjects to schools.

Listening Practice

 Listen and write.

  MP3 J3-11

Pius Mau Piailug

Pius "Mau" Piailug was born in 1932 on Satawal, a small island in the nation of Micronesia. He learned traditional methods for ¹_____ that were used before GPS and maps. Instead, Mau looked at the stars, clouds, winds, water movements, and even animals to know his location and his direction. By the age of 18, he had become a "palu," a master in traditional sailing techniques. As Mau grew older, the lifestyle of his people on Satawal began to change. Young people were going to newly-built schools to learn Western subjects, and traditional life began to disappear and be forgotten. This made Mau worried. In order to ²_____ the value of traditional sailing techniques, he teamed up with some researchers to sail from Hawaii to Tahiti using only the knowledge he received in his village. No modern technology would be used. The trip took 34 days, but it was successful. This proved that ³_____ people could travel long ⁴_____ without maps or computers. In addition, ⁵_____ traditional Micronesian and Polynesian culture ⁶_____ after the trip. Mau's efforts helped save knowledge from many centuries from disappearing forever, and people still celebrate his efforts today.

Word Bank

proof	prove	distances
interest in	interesting	sail in
incresed	increased	sailing
ancient	distences	anchient

 Listen. Pause. Say each sentence.

  MP3 J3-11G

Writing Practice

 Write the words.

1 _____

n moving in a boat on water

2 _____

v show for sure

3 _____

v go up

4 _____

adj from a long time ago

5 _____

n a long space

6 _____ X

n caring about X

ex When people have an _____ X, they care about X.

 Write the words in each blank.

Summary

Pius Mau Piailug _____ a "palu," a master of traditional _____ techniques that were used before GPS and _____. He teamed up with some _____ to sail using only traditional methods, saving traditional knowledge from disappearing forever.

Word Puzzle

 Complete the word puzzle.

1 ↓

caring about X

When people have an
_____ X, they care
about X.

2 ↓

a long space

3 →

from a long time ago

5 ↓

go up

4 →

moving in a boat on water

6 →

show for sure

UNIT 12

Mary Anning

Teacher's Book p.232

Have you ever heard of Mary Anning?
Look at the illustration.
What do you think Anning was known for?

Mary Anning was born in 1799 in a small English town near the sea called Lyme Regis. Her family was very poor, and her father died when she was still young. In order to make money for her family, she would walk along the beach looking for things that she could sell. One day, Anning and her brother were at some cliffs when they found a skeleton. At first they thought it was a crocodile, but they realized it was an animal they had never seen. Mary Anning and her brother had found an *ichthyosaur* fossil. It was the largest and most complete one found at that time. Mary Anning found many more fossils in the cliffs, and the area became known as the "Jurassic Coast." In the early 1800s, people were only starting to research dinosaurs. Mary Anning dug up and traded them, making her very important in the beginning of *paleontology*. She never studied the subject in school, but she knew more about fossils than many of the scientists of the time. However, because she was a woman, many male scientists looked down on her and stole her research. It was not until many decades after her death that the importance of Mary Anning's work was recognized.

New Words

skeleton

n all the bones of a body

cliff

n a very steep side of a mountain

fossil

n a bone, skeleton, or print from a very very old being

dig up

v get out of the earth

trade

v buy and sell or exchange

look down on X

v think X is not important or good

Part A. Sentence Completion

1. A: Where did they find your wallet?
   B: My sister and her friend _____ just walking down the street and saw it.

   (A) has
   (B) was
   (C) have
   (D) were

2. A: Why should I listen to you about history?
   B: Hey! I know more about it _____ you do.

   (A) as
   (B) for
   (C) than
   (D) when

Part B. Situational Writing

3.

   Mr. Perez is standing near the edge of the _____.

   (A) cliff
   (B) wall
   (C) table
   (D) water

4.

   The team is digging up _____.

   (A) fossils
   (B) scales
   (C) crystals
   (D) diamonds

Long Necked Dinosaurs (Sauropods)

Dreadnoughtus
- Head and neck = 12.2m
- Total length = 26m
- Named after huge battleships
- Lived 77 million years ago

- Long necks
- Recently discovered
- Land-based
- Plant eaters
- Four thick legs

Qijianglong
- 15m long
- Neck filled with air
- Lived about 160 million years ago

5. According to the diagram, which dinosaur got its name from a type of ship?

(A) the dreadnoughtus
(B) the qijianglong
(C) both
(D) neither

6. According to the diagram, which of the following is true?

(A) Both dinosaurs were meat eaters.
(B) Both dinosaurs were discovered in the 19th century.
(C) The qijianglong lived on the earth more recently than the dreadnoughtus.
(D) The qijianglong's body is longer than the dreadnoughtus' head and neck.

Part D. General Reading and Retelling

Mary Anning was born in 1799 in a small English town near the sea called Lyme Regis. Her family was very poor, and her father died when she was still young. In order to make money for her family, she would walk along the beach looking for things that she could sell. One day, Anning and her brother were at some cliffs when they found a skeleton. At first they thought it was a crocodile, but they realized it was an animal they had never seen. Mary Anning and her brother had found an *ichthyosaur* fossil. It was the largest and most complete one found at that time. Mary Anning found many more fossils in the cliffs, and the area became known as the "Jurassic Coast." In the early 1800s, people were only starting to research dinosaurs. Mary Anning dug up and traded them, making her very important in the beginning of *paleontology*. She never studied the subject in school, but she knew more about fossils than many of the scientists of the time. However, because she was a woman, many male scientists looked down on her and stole her research. It was not until many decades after her death that the importance of Mary Anning's work was recognized.

7. According to the passage, which is true about Mary Anning?

   (A) She was born in 1788.
   (B) She came from a town near the sea.
   (C) Her mother died when Anning was young.
   (D) Her family was among the richest in town.

8. According to the passage, what did Anning and her brother think the fossil was at first?

   (A) a turtle
   (B) a jellyfish
   (C) a crocodile
   (D) an elephant

9. According to the passage, what was the "Jurassic Coast"?

   (A) a cliff area with many fossils
   (B) a museum with dinosaur displays
   (C) an ocean beach with pretty shells
   (D) an amusement park started by Anning

10. Which of the following is most likely a reason Anning's work was not recognized?

   (A) She buried the fossils.
   (B) Men stole her research.
   (C) Anning only studied in school.
   (D) People thought dinosaurs were boring.

Listen and write.

MP3 J3-12

Mary Anning

Mary Anning was born in 1799 in a small English town near the sea called Lyme Regis. Her family was very poor, and her father died when she was still young. In order to make money for her family, she would walk along the beach looking for things that she could sell. One day, Anning and her brother were at some ¹ _____ when they found a ² _____ . At first they thought it was a crocodile, but they realized it was an animal they had never seen. Mary Anning and her brother had found an *ichthyosaur* fossil. It was the largest and most complete one found at that time. Mary Anning found many more ³ _____ in the cliffs, and the area became known as the "Jurassic Coast." In the early 1800s, people were only starting to research dinosaurs. Mary Anning ⁴ _____ and ⁵ _____ them, making her very important in the beginning of *paleontology*. She never studied the subject in school, but she knew more about fossils than many of the scientists of the time. However, because she was a woman, many male scientists looked down ⁶ _____ and stole her research. It was not until many decades after her death that the importance of Mary Anning's work was recognized.

Word Bank

traded	dug up	onner
skelton	skeleton	fossil
on her	cliffs	dugup
traited	clifs	fossils

Listen. Pause. Say each sentence.

MP3 J3-12G

Writing Practice

 Write the words.

1 _____

[n] all the bones of a body

2 _____

[n] a very steep side of a mountain

3 _____

[n] a bone, skeleton, or print from a very very old being

4 _____

[v] get out of the earth

5 _____

[v] buy and sell or exchange

6 _____ X

[v] think X is not important or good

📄 Write the words in each blank.

Summary

Mary Anning found, researched, and traded _____. However, because she was a woman, many male scientists looked _____ on her and stole her research. The importance of her _____ was acknowledged many _____ after her death.

Word Puzzle

 Complete the word puzzle.

2 ↓
a bone, skeleton, or print from a very very old being

1 →
a very steep side of a mountain

4 ↓
think X is not important or good

3 →
all the bones of a body

6 →
get out of the earth

5 ↓
buy and sell or exchange

Agatha Christie's
Mysterious Disappearance

Teacher's Book
p.237

The biggest prize for writers of mystery stories is the "The Agatha Award," named after the famous author, Agatha Christie. Christie's work life was all about writing incredible mystery stories. However, her personal life was also filled with mystery—in particular, the mystery of the author's disappearance.

On December 3, 1926, Christie left home in her car. The next day the car was discovered hanging over a cliff. In it were Christie's fur coat and driver's licence, but no Christie. Over one thousand police officers and 15,000 volunteers searched for the missing writer, but they could not find her. Rumors started to go around. One rumor was that Christie had disappeared to advertise her novels. Another rumor was that Christie was hiding in London disguised in men's clothing. Eventually, Christie appeared. She was at a hotel in the countryside.

Christie said she could not remember anything that had happened during the ten days she was missing. However, when she checked in at the hotel she used the name "Theresa Neele." Later, after Christie and her husband had divorced, it turned out that her husband had had a girlfriend. That girlfriend's name was Theresa Neele.

Some people think Christie really could not remember what happened. Others think that Christie crashed her car on purpose. In fact, nobody really knows why Agatha Christie disappeared for ten days in 1926.

ANSWERS

UNIT 1
J3-1
p.11

	1 (B)	2 (D)	3 (B)	4 (D)	5 (D)	6 (C)	7 (B)	8 (C)	9 (B)	10 (B)
🎧	1 chemistry	2 experiments	3 materials	4 molecules	5 nuclear	6 disagreed				
✏️	1 chemistry	2 experiment	3 material	4 molecule	5 diagree with	6 nuclear weapon				

📄 chemistry, Nobel, nuclear, disagreed

→ 1 experiment 5 material 6 molecule ↓ 2 nuclear weapon 3 disagree with 4 chemistry

UNIT 2
J3-2
p.19

	1 (D)	2 (D)	3 (D)	4 (A)	5 (A)	6 (C)	7 (D)	8 (A)	9 (C)	10 (C)
🎧	1 fascinating	2 geometry	3 imaginary	4 surfaces	5 billiard	6 ground-breaking				
✏️	1 geometry	2 fascinating	3 imaginary	4 surface	5 billiard ball	6 ground-breaking				

📄 mathematician, Medal, first, cancer

→ 3 imaginary 5 surface 6 fascinating ↓ 1 billiard ball 2 ground-breaking 4 geometry

UNIT 3
J3-3
p.27

	1 (B)	2 (C)	3 (D)	4 (B)	5 (A)	6 (C)	7 (C)	8 (A)	9 (D)	10 (C)
🎧	1 advanced	2 scholarship	3 particles	4 revolutionary	5 establish	6 institutes				
✏️	1 advance	2 scholarship	3 particle	4 revolutionary	5 establish	6 institute				

📄 effect, clear, revolutionary, Physics

→ 4 establish 6 advance ↓ 1 particle 2 scholarship 3 revolutionary 5 institute

UNIT 4
J3-4
p.35

	1 (D)	2 (B)	3 (B)	4 (C)	5 (D)	6 (C)	7 (D)	8 (D)	9 (D)	10 (C)
🎧	1 hired	2 subjects	3 passion	4 invention	5 automatically	6 potential				
✏️	1 hire	2 subject	3 have a deep passion for	4 invention	5 automatically	6 saw the potential of				

📄 computer, potential, engine, programs

→ 5 saw the potential of 6 subject ↓ 1 invention 2 automatically 3 hire 4 have a deep passion for

UNIT 5
J3-5
p.45

	1 (B)	2 (B)	3 (B)	4 (B)	5 (D)	6 (C)	7 (B)	8 (C)	9 (B)	10 (D)
🎧	1 respect	2 recovered	3 cure for	4 boiled	5 soaked	6 humanity				
✏️	1 respect	2 recover	3 cure for	4 boil	5 soak	6 humanity				

📄 medicine, cure, research, plant

→ 1 recover 4 humanity 5 boil ↓ 1 respect 2 soak 3 cure for

UNIT 6
J3-6
p.53

	1 (A)	2 (B)	3 (C)	4 (B)	5 (D)	6 (B)	7 (C)	8 (B)	9 (C)	10 (D)
🎧	1 hostile	2 escape	3 protect	4 rights	5 representative	6 impact				
✏️	1 hostile	2 escape	3 protect	4 rights	5 representative for	6 have an impact on				

📄 save, Guatemala, war, impact

→ 4 hostile 5 escape 6 have an impact on ↓ 1 rights 2 protect 3 representative for

UNIT 7
J3-7
p.61

	1 (C)	2 (B)	3 (B)	4 (A)	5 (C)	6 (A)	7 (D)	8 (B)	9 (A)	10 (B)
🎧	1 plans	2 original	3 later on	4 curve	5 unusual	6 unique				
✏️	1 plans	2 original	3 later on	4 curve	5 unusual	6 unique				

📄 architects, buildings, unique, creativity

→ 2 unusual 5 unique 6 original ↓ 1 plans 3 later on 4 curve

UNIT 8
J3-8
p.69

	1 (D)	2 (D)	3 (D)	4 (D)	5 (B)	6 (D)	7 (D)	8 (A)	9 (B)	10 (B)
🎧	1 activist	2 veterinarians	3 founded	4 thanks	5 soil	6 influence				
✏️	1 activist	2 veterinarian	3 found	4 thanks to	5 soil	6 influence others				

📄 environment, Belt, influence, trees

→ 1 activist 3 veterinarian 5 found 6 soil ↓ 2 thanks to 4 influence others

UNIT 9
J3-9
p.79

	1 (B)	2 (B)	3 (A)	4 (D)	5 (B)	6 (B)	7 (C)	8 (B)	9 (B)	10 (C)
🎧	1 quality	2 spaceships	3 Eventually	4 trained	5 head of	6 opportunities				
✏️	1 bad in quality	2 spaceship	3 eventually	4 train to	5 head of	6 opportunity				

📄 woman, head, opportunities, space

→ 2 spaceship 6 eventually ↓ 1 opportunity 3 bad in quality 4 train to 5 head of

UNIT 10
J3-10
p.87

	1 (B)	2 (D)	3 (B)	4 (D)	5 (D)	6 (D)	7 (C)	8 (C)	9 (B)	10 (B)
🎧	1 generals	2 took over	3 based	4 bestseller	5 translated	6 worldwide				
✏️	1 general	2 take over	3 be based on	4 bestseller	5 translate	6 worldwide				

📄 authors, book, translated, languages

→ 5 translate 6 take over ↓ 1 be based on 2 bestseller 3 worldwide 4 general

UNIT 11
J3-11
p.95

	1 (B)	2 (D)	3 (A)	4 (C)	5 (C)	6 (A)	7 (C)	8 (B)	9 (C)	10 (C)
🎧	1 sailing	2 prove	3 ancient	4 distances	5 interest in	6 increased				
✏️	1 sailing	2 prove	3 increase	4 ancient	5 long distance	6 interest in				

📄 was, sailing, maps, researchers

→ 3 ancient 4 sailing 6 prove ↓ 1 interest in 2 long distance 5 increase

UNIT 12
J3-12
p.103

	1 (D)	2 (C)	3 (A)	4 (A)	5 (A)	6 (D)	7 (B)	8 (C)	9 (A)	10 (B)
🎧	1 cliffs	2 skeleton	3 fossils	4 dug up	5 traded	6 on her				
✏️	1 skeleton	2 cliff	3 fossil	4 dig up	5 trade	6 look down on				

📄 fossils, down, work, decades

→ 1 cliff 3 skeleton 6 dig up ↓ 2 fossil 4 look down on 5 trade